Teach Your Granny to Text & Other Ways to Change the World

we are what we do ©

Produced by Nick Stanhope
Art direction and design by New Future Graphic
Written by Tanis Taylor...
& 4,386 children (more or less)

WALKER
BOOKS

✳ SHORT BOOKS

About We Are What We Do

We Are What We Do is a global social change movement. We believe it is not just politicians, institutions and big business that change the world – it is also ordinary people like you and me. Our job is to bring people together and demonstrate how, using simple, everyday actions, we can create a global movement of doing and changing; *doing* small actions and *changing* big problems.

We started back in 2003 with the simple question, "What would you ask one million people to do to change the world?" We received thousands of suggestions from all over the globe and the result was our book, *Change the World for a Fiver – 50 actions to change the world and make you feel good*.

The first action was "decline plastic bags whenever possible" – such a small action and one that everyone could do to make a positive contribution to our environment. So why weren't they? we wondered. We asked handbag and accessories designer Anya Hindmarch to help. Together we created the "I'm NOT a plastic bag" bag. People saw it. And cottoned on. Millions of people.

We've done loads of other things too – you can find out all about them at our website:

www.wearewhatwedo.org

We've seen the power of small actions. How they can change the big things. And if there was ever a time to be changing big things it is now. As Mahatma Gandhi said, "We must be the change we want to see in the world."

Who are we?
We Are What We Do.

you have a SUPER POWER

It's not as whizzy as X-ray vision or flying.
In fact as super powers go it's pretty ordinary.
But if you use it, you can change things.

BIG THINGS!

Like global warming, bullying, animal rights
and why people don't smile more. Curious?

You do things, every day. Small things. Let's call them **"actions"**. You take showers. You eat chicken nuggets. You buy stuff. You fart.

Over your lifetime these actions add up. You will spend **6,000 hours in the shower**. You will eat **1,201 chickens** (or nutloaves if you're a veggie). You will buy **678,740 things**. (Wow!) And you will fart **421,575 times**. (Now that's not to be sniffed at.)

You have a HUGE impact on the world around you. Every day, your actions and your choices influence things – from your mates and your mum, to chicken farmers and factory workers in Africa. **This is your super power.** The power to change things. Just a bit. Every day. And when lots and lots of us make small changes to our everyday actions we can…

CHANGE THE WORLD

COR! AMAZING!

small actions ×
lots of people = BIG CHANGE

What are these actions? What are the things that will make a difference?

We asked the most imaginative people we knew. We asked you. And here they are. Thirty amazing, everyday actions. By children. For children. Actions that everyone can do. To change the world.

They are small. They are strange.
But do them with others and things will change.

Go on. Get stuck in. Try Erica's Action 15 and teach your granny to text. Why? Because when you do it, you get to spend time with someone from another generation. Because if we all did it there would be millions of grandparents who could stay in touch better. Because you know stuff. And grans know stuff. And because we should all swap stuff. (Thanks Erica. Our title would be pants without you.) Unplug Sammah's Action 22. Pump up Omar's Action 29. Give away Emma's Action 20. And when you're done, pester everyone you know into doing YOUR amazing everyday Action 30.

Welcome to your SUPER POWER

Use it wisely. And you can change anything and everything that matters to you – from how your house recycles and how green your teacher is, to fat dads and gloomy mates.

Start here … continue online and out there and who knows where it will end. Happy world-changing!

Make someone smile

Q: What colour is a burp?
A: Burple

There are some people who hardly ever smile. You could call them grumpy-lumps. We call them challenges.

Make someone smile – for no reason in particular.

Fact: It takes half as many muscles to smile as it does to frown.

THANK YOU FOR MY LOVELY PASTA TEA X

How do you catch a squirrel?

Climb a tree and act like a nut!

You see 300 people every day. If one million kids smile at 300 people each, every person in Britain will get smiled at. Five times.

VISITOR

I saw this and I thought of you X

YO, WHATS UP?

Walk your dad

Like dogs, grown-ups get cranky when they stay indoors all 🕐 DAY Long. Unlike dogs - who walk an average of 676 miles a year - dads walk just 197. KEEP them Off the furniture: tAKe a grown-up for A WALK.

11

Grow something & eat it

Take this boring bit of paper and turn it into something amazing. Go on. Dare you.

INSTRUCTIONS

Basil loves the sun and grows well indoors. Its favourite spot is a sunny windowsill in the kitchen.

FIRST: Find or make a good container with some holes in the bottom.

NEXT: Fill it with nice soil.

THEN: Soak the paper in water and pop it in the pot a few centimetres under the soil.

CARE: Keep the soil wet, but not drenched in water.

HOME GROWN FOOD

It's easy! It's free!
It's amazing!!
No wasteful packaging!
No supermarket queues!
WARNING:
May contain bugs.

BLIMEY! It's growing!
HOORAY!! Within a couple
of weeks you should see
something. As soon as
there are plenty of leaves,
pinch them off and scatter
them on top of Action 10.

13

Stand up for something

If a friend was being bullied you could wait for someone else to do something.

If your school wasn't recycling you could wait for your Head to do something.

If the planet was heating up you could wait for the government to do something.

Personally, we hate waiting.

Speak up.

Change your world.

Starting from now.

STOP GAN

SAY N TO CH LABO

PETE'S MY MATE, LEAVE HIM ALONE

SAVE THE BUMB

I'm standing up for...

Photography: Stephen Morgan

Switch things off when you leave the room

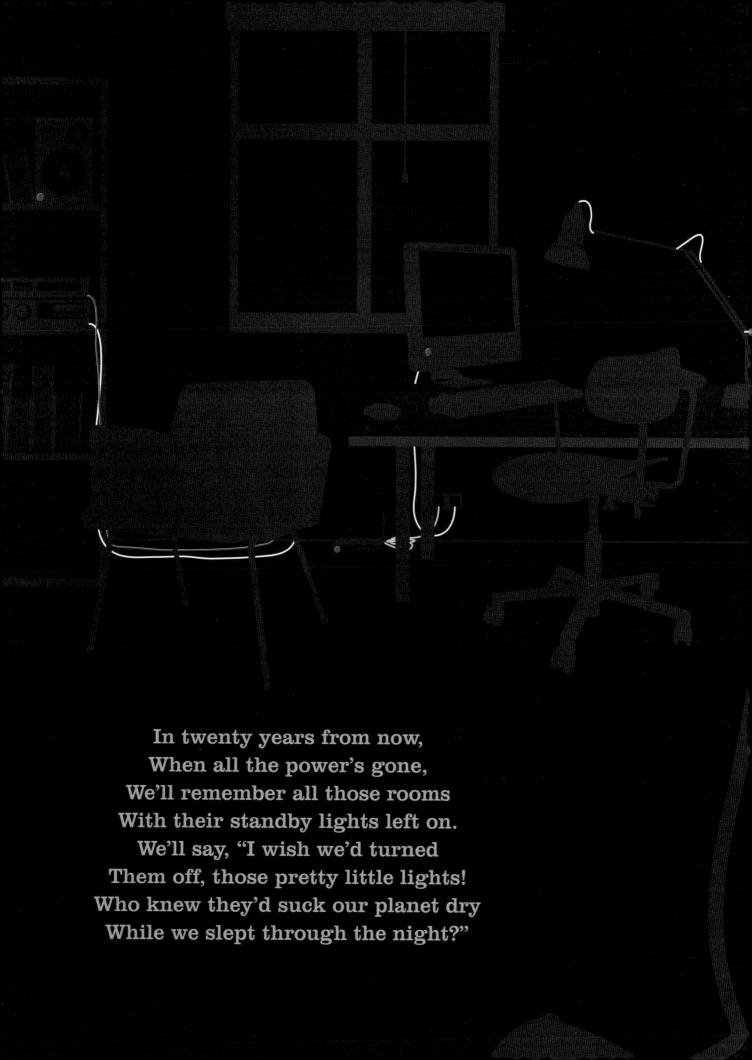

In twenty years from now,
When all the power's gone,
We'll remember all those rooms
With their standby lights left on.
We'll say, "I wish we'd turned
Them off, those pretty little lights!
Who knew they'd suck our planet dry
While we slept through the night?"

Test your teacher

FED UP WITH BEING TESTED BY YOUR TEACHER? LET'S SEE HOW THEY LIKE IT.

SEE HOW THEY DO IN _YOUR_ FAVOURITE SUBJECT – PLANET SAVING. MOSTLY Cs? NOT GOOD ENOUGH. CHALLENGE THEM TO IMPROVE, THEN TEST THEM AGAIN.

"WHAT IS IT MISS, ANOTHER TOILET BREAK?" _SIGH_ "DIDN'T YOU JUST HAVE ONE?"

THE BIG GREEN TEST FOR TEACHERS

Tick the boxes to indicate your answers

1 At home

a. How many of your lightbulbs are low-energy?
- A. All
- B. Some
- C. None

b. What temperature do you normally wash your clothes on?
- A. 30°
- B. 40°
- C. 50°+

c. Are you a composter?
- A. Yes
- B. No
- C. A what?!

d. How often do you leave things on stand-by?
- A. Never
- B. Sometimes
- C. Always

e. Do you charge your mobile phone overnight?
- A. Never
- B. Sometimes
- C. Always

f. Do you turn the tap off when you brush your teeth?
- A. Always
- B. When I remember!
- C. Never

2 Travelling about

a. How do you travel to school?
- A. Walk, cycle, on public transport
- B. In a full car of people
- C. In a car on my own

b. Do you check that your tyres are pumped up to the right pressure levels? (helps your car use less fuel!)
- A. Regularly
- B. Occasionally
- C. Never

c. How do you travel if your journey's less than a mile?
- A. Walk or cycle
- B. Public transport
- C. Car

d. How many flights do you take every year?
- A. None
- B. One or two
- C. More than three

3 At school

a. Do you use both sides of the paper when you photocopy?
- A. Always
- B. Sometimes
- C. Never

b. Do you have recycling bins in the staff room?
- A. Yes, for everything!
- B. Yes, for paper
- C. No, none

c. How much water do you boil to make a cup of tea?
- A. Just as much as I need
- B. A bit more than I need
- C. A full kettle almost always

d. Do you print on recycled paper?
- A. Always
- B. Sometimes
- C. Never

4 How did you score?

Mostly As: Bright Green. Well done. Hats off. You are qualified to teach me in the ways of the world as you are a big, green, shining beacon. Teacher, I salute you

Mostly Bs: Light Green. You might know your stuff in the classroom, but you won't win any prizes for planet-saving. Strong start, but must try harder

Mostly Cs: Limp Green. Oh dear, we have a problem. If this doesn't improve, not only will the planet go "pop", but you will have to see me after class

Look closer

Sometimes it pays to take your time. To look closer, to find the things no one else does. It makes you good at Where's Wally? It makes you good at life.

Ten of our actions have wandered into Wally's world. Can you find them? (And him).

Be friendly in sign language

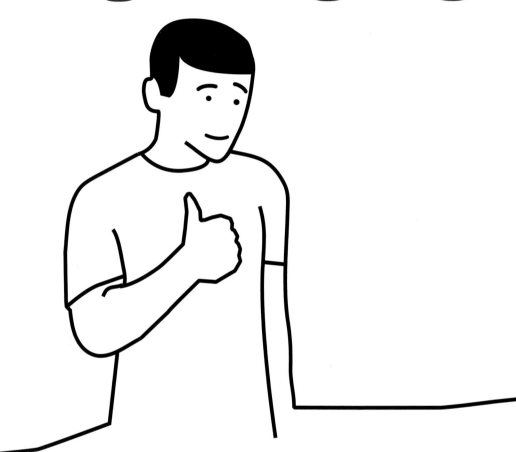

"Alright?"

A bit of sign language always comes in handy. Use it in quiet places (libraries). Use it in loud places (football matches). Use it to make 9 million new friends.*

Illustration: New Future Graphic

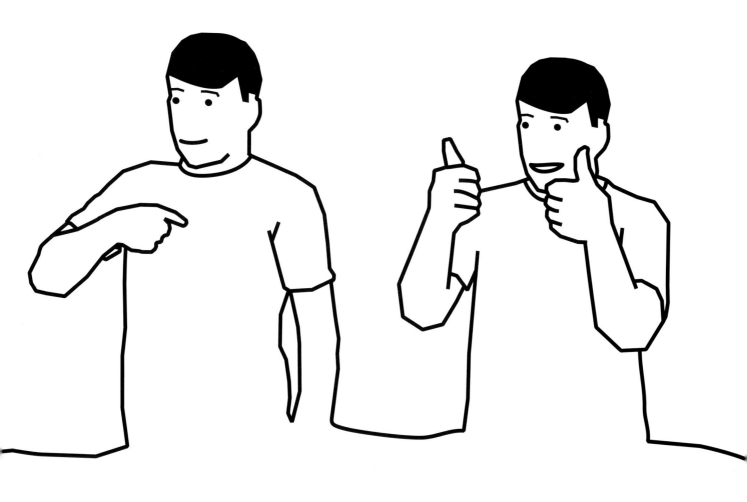

"I'm fantastic!"

* There are estimated to be about 9
  million deaf and hard of hearing people
  in the UK. And more than 34,000 deaf
  children and young people.

Layer up

What is our greatest weapon against global warming?

Science? Biofuel? Solar power?

Nu-huh. It's the sweater. The next time it gets chilly, put a sweater on.

Not the heating.

In 1970 the average temperature of a British house was 12°C. Today it is 19°C.

Illustration: Marcus Walters

Is your central heating making you fat? When our houses are cooler our bodies burn calories and keep us nice and toasty.

The first radiator was invented in 1855. Before that people wore bigger jumpers. And hugged more.

Cook a meal from scratch

Your mission, should you choose to accept it, is dinner for two. Cook it from scratch. Using only raw ingredients.

Your secret weapon? Sam Stern, teenage chef. Good luck.

(And call us when it's ready)

MARGHERITA PIZZA - SERVES 2

PIZZA BASE :

450 g/1lb STRONG WHITE
BREAD FLOUR
1 TSP SALT
1 TSP CASTER SUGAR
2 x 7G SACHET FAST ACTION
DRIED YEAST
300 ML / ½ PINT WARM WATER
2 TSPS GOOD OLIVE OIL

PIZZA TOPPING :
2 x 150g BALL MOZZARELLA
1 x 400g CAN
CHOPPED TOMATOES

1 CLOVE GARLIC,
CRUSHED

FEW BLACK OLIVES
SALT AND BLACK PEPPER
OLIVE OIL

A FEW LEAVES OF
ACTION 03

SAM'S MARGHERITA PIZZA

1. SIFT FLOUR AND SALT INTO A BOWL. ADD SUGAR AND YEAST.

2. POUR IN WATER AND OLIVE OIL. WORK DOUGH INTO A SOFT BALL. ADD A DROP MORE WATER IF NEEDED.

3. SLAP DOUGH ONTO A LIGHTLY FLOURED BOARD. PUNCH, PULL, THUMP AND KNEAD FOR 10 MIN UNTIL SOFT AND ELASTIC.

4. LEAVE COVERED IN A WARM PLACE FOR 1 HOUR, OR UNTIL DOUBLED IN SIZE.

5. LIGHTLY OIL TWO BAKING TRAYS. DIVIDE DOUGH INTO TWO EQUAL BALLS AND ROLL OUT FLAT. LEAVE COVERED ON BAKING TRAYS TO RISE AGAIN FOR 15 MINS.

6. PREHEAT OVEN TO 230°C/400°F/GAS 6

7. MIX GARLIC INTO CHOPPED TOMATO, SPREAD ON BASE.

8. CHUCK ON SLICED MOZZARELLA, OLIVES, SEASONING. DRIZZLE WITH A LITTLE OLIVE OIL.

9. BAKE 15-20 MIN. SERVE WITH A SCATTERING OF ACTION 03.

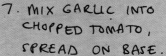

Love your stuff

New stuff comes in nice packaging.

It smells good and has fancy tags.

Old stuff doesn't. It's flat from being at the bottom of your bed. Or smelly from being your favourite football shirt. It's full of holes.

And you've earned every one of them.

Love your stuff. To bits.

I love snakey cos he scares my brother

I have had her for a long time

I love taking pictures of things that I love

I've had it since I was a baby

This turtle reminds me of my granddad

He's got good clothes

It reminds me of being in Portugal

Football is my best subject

I love Tom because I got him When I was a baby

I will always love her.

He can be moody but dont care.

She is always happy

Because we have good hugs.

This is my first trophy.

Photography: Malcolm Menzies & WAWWD

APRIL

Children's Day
This day is celebrated throughout Turkey to remind people that children are the future. Turkish children dress in national dress and perform in plays and musicals, and the seats in parliament are held by children for one day only.

Add your own...

Vaisakhi
One of the most important holidays in the Sikh calendar, this is a time to remember the birth of Sikhism in 1699. People clean and decorate their local Gudwaras, (the Sikh place of worship), with flowers, and bathe themselves to purify body and soul before celebrating with parades, dancing and singing. Children start the practice of charity on this day and continue it throughout the year.

Pesach
Pesach or "Passover" is an eight-day feast celebrating the end of slavery for the Jewish people when they fled Egypt, and their arrival in Israel. People eat "matzo", a flatbread, to remind them that when they left Egypt it was in such a rush that their bread didn't have time to rise.

MAY

Cheese Rolling
Since the nineteenth-century, competitors in Gloucestershire have taken part in this event: a round of Double Gloucester cheese is rolled from the top of a steep hill and they all try to catch it. Since the cheese can reach speeds of 70mph, this is quite a challenge!

Add your own...

Baby-Jumping Festival
In the village of Castrillo de Murcia in Spain, grown men dressed as devils leap over a row of helpless babies! As they jump they take all the evil with them and cleanse the children.

Vesak
The most important event of the Buddhist calendar, Vesak, or Buddha's Day, celebrates the Buddha's birth, death and enlightenment. Homes are cleaned and decorated. Flowers, candles and joss-sticks are left at the feet of statues. People eat vegetarian food and caged animals, insects and birds are ceremonially freed.

JUNE

Summer Solstice
Solstice comes from the Latin for "sun stands still" and the Summer Solstice is when the sun is at its highest elevation of the year. The Celts celebrated with bonfires to add to the sun's energy and in the UK today, pagans and druids dance and light fires to greet the sunrise at Stonehenge's stone circle.

Dragon Boat Festival
When a famous Chinese poet called Qu Yuan was drowned, the townsfolk took to their boats, beating drums and throwing dumplings into the water to scare away fish and stop creatures from eating his body. Today, teams of twenty-two paddlers take to the water in long dragon boats and race to the sound of drums.

Add your own...

JANUARY

Burns' night
A Scottish celebration of the life of poet Robert Burns on 25th January (Robert Burns wrote "Auld Lang Syne". All together now...).

Add your own...

Add your own...

The Lantern Festival
On the fifteenth day of the first month the streets are lit with glowing, colourful lanterns to mark the end of the Chinese New Year and welcome new beginnings. Children stroll the streets holding home-made lanterns.

Up Helly Aa
A festival held in the Shetlands to celebrate the end of wintertime on the 24th day after Christmas. Festive folk dress up and walk through the town to their Viking ship!

FEBRUARY

Groundhog Day
If the groundhog (also known as a woodchuck or ground squirrel) emerges from his burrow on 2nd February and doesn't see his shadow, it means winter will soon end. If he does see his shadow, it's back into his hole, and winter for six more weeks... Boo.

Rissun
This Shinto celebration on 3rd February marks the end of winter and the chasing away of evil spirits. People throw handfuls of beans into any dark corners while shouting, "Fortune in, Devils out!"

BEANS

Add your own...

Carnival
Four days before Ash Wednesday every year, the streets of Rio de Janeiro, Brazil, come alive with parties, festivals and samba bands. The crowds wear colourful outfits covered with feathers and sequins, and children practise for months to perform in dancing bands.

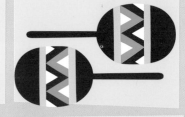

MARCH

St David's Day
Saint David is the patron saint of Wales and 1st March is his feast day. People celebrate Welsh culture and history and wear daffodils or leeks in their lapels.

Doll's Festival
A day for girls! In Japan young girls display dolls in traditional dress on a platform in their house. Throughout the festival, families visit shrines to pray for girls' health and happiness.

Add your own...

Holi
This Hindu festival from India is nicknamed the "Festival of Colours" because during the day people spill out onto the streets and throw huge amounts of coloured powder and water at each other!

Go to more parties

Merry Bean-Throwing Day!

Happy Diwali!

Groundhog Greetings!

The great thing about having friends from other cultures is that you get to go to all their parties.

We've taken the liberty of putting a few dates in your diary.

Now go fill in the rest.

Illustration: Andreas Samuelsson

OCTOBER

Halloween
Legend has it that, on 31st October, the boundary between the dead and the living gets blurred. So to confuse those dastardly spirits, dress as a ghoul yourself! Boo.

Oktoberfest
A jolly German festival where the women wear a traditional outfit called a "dirndl" and men wear "lederhosen" or leather trousers. Meat is eaten, beer is drunk and there is much singing and good cheer.

Add your own...

Diwali
Diwali is the Festival of Light, celebrated by Sikhs, Hindus and Jains. In Britain, as in India, the festival is a time for spring-cleaning the home, for wearing new clothes and, most importantly, for decorating buildings with lights.

NOVEMBER

Monkey Buffet
In Thailand, locals gather together and lay on a magnificent buffet of fruit and vegetables for the monkeys that roam free. Around 600 of them turn up to take advantage of this free meal!

Day of the Dead
Mexican people pray to the souls of dead relatives on this day and ask them to return for one night. They decorate their homes with skulls, dress as skeletons and parade through the streets. Bread is even baked in the shape of a skull! This festival remembers dead relatives and celebrates their lives.

Add your own...

DECEMBER

Christmas
An annual Christian holiday that celebrates the birth of Jesus. Children receive gifts and cards from Santa Claus and Christmas trees are dressed with baubles and decorations and topped with a star to represent the Star of Bethlehem from the Nativity story.

Santa Lucia
On 13th December, one of winter's longest, darkest nights, girls in Sweden dress up as Santa Lucia in a white dress and a crown of candles. The day is a big feast day and boys may dress as gingerbread men while sweet Lucia buns are eaten in celebration.

Add your own...

JULY

World Pillow Fighting Championships

Competitors sit, facing each other, on the top of a slippery pole above a mud-pit. Using only a pillow they must unseat their opponent. Rounds last one minute. Feathers will fly.

Alien Festival

Legend has it that a UFO crashed in Roswell, New Mexico, USA, in 1947 and each year people dressed as aliens go there to parade and party. The truth is out there… somewhere.

Add your own...

Grandmothers' Festival

A grand old celebration of grandmothers in Norway. This festival sees grannies riding motorbikes and racehorses, skydiving and scuba diving.

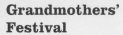
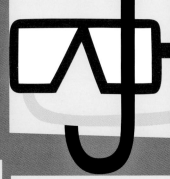

AUGUST

Tomato Fight

The biggest food fight in the world, this Spanish festival involves 110,000 kilos of tomatoes being thrown at anyone you can manage to hit. "Hey slowcoach, ketchup!"

Highland Games

What better way to celebrate Scotland than these games that came down from the Highlands. Cabers (long pine logs) are tossed and heavy stones thrown while bagpipes are played and kilts worn.

Add your own...

Raksha Bandhan

A Hindu festival for brothers and sisters marked by the tying of a holy thread, by the sister, onto the wrist of her brother. In return the brother promises to look after her and they feed each other sweets. (No brother, no worries! Any male can be "adopted" as a brother for the occasion.)

SEPTEMBER

Add your own...

Ramadan

Ramadan is a month of fasting from sunrise to sunset. During Ramadan, Muslims pray and fast, celebrating the time when the verses of the Qur'an were revealed to the Prophet Muhammad. The Islamic holiday of Eid marks the end of Ramadan.

Ethiopian New Year's Day

The start of the New Year in Ethiopia on 11th September is a colourful affair, with priests walking around their churches with bright umbrellas and colourful holy books. Rastafarians believe Ethiopia is their spiritual homeland, so they celebrate this too.

Ask "Why?"

Years ago someone looked up into the night sky and asked: "Why can't we build something powerful enough to take man to the moon?" The rest, as they say, is history.

WHY DO WE HAVE SCHOOL?

WHY IS THE SKY BLUE?

WHY DO WE WALK UPRIGHT?

WHY DO CHILDREN STILL DIE OF HUNGER WHEN THERE IS ENOUGH FOOD IN THE WORLD?

WHY DO SOME PEOPLE GROW TALLER THAN OTHERS?

WHY ISN'T EVERYONE THE SAME RELIGION?

WHY DO WE REMEMBER SOME THINGS AND NOT OTHERS? WHY DO CROCODILES EAT ROCKS?

Illustration: Marcus Walters

Love where you live

Maps can be boring. This one won't be.
Maps can be full of places that everyone
knows. This one won't be.

This is your map. Fill it with the
stuff that only you know. Fill it with
the stuff that other kids would
actually want to know.

Put your neighbourhood
on the map.

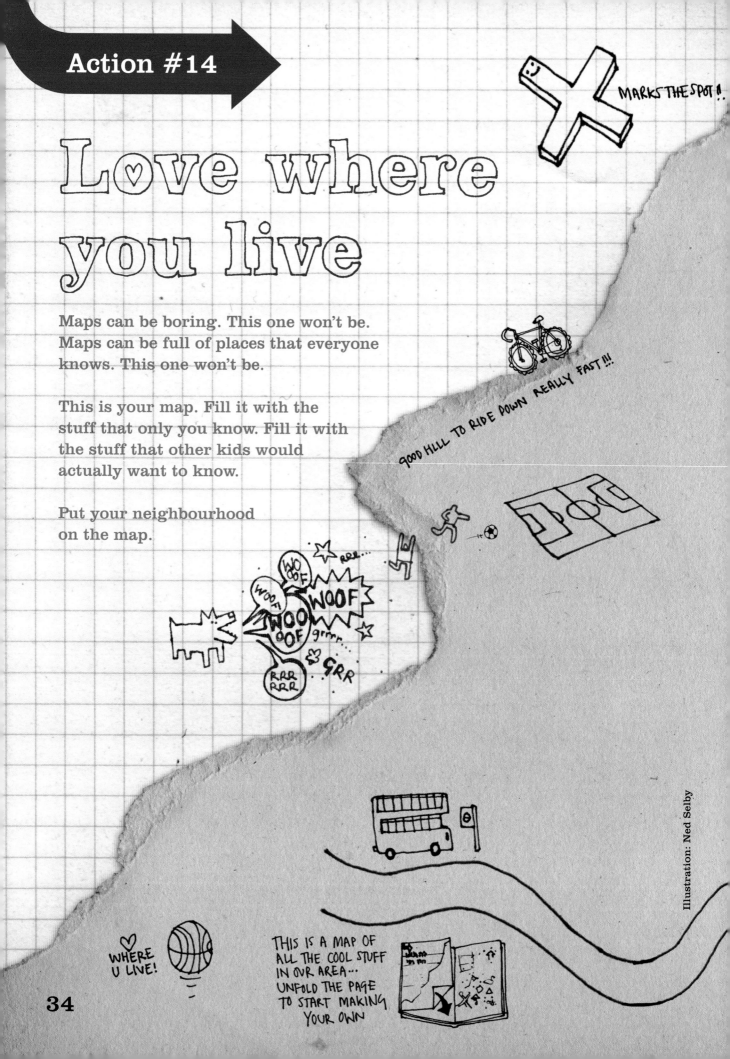

MARKS THE SPOT!!

GOOD HILL TO RIDE DOWN REALLY FAST!!!

WOOF WOOF WOO OOF RRR... WOOF grrrr... GRR RRR RRR

WHERE U LIVE!

THIS IS A MAP OF
ALL THE COOL STUFF
IN OUR AREA...
UNFOLD THE PAGE
TO START MAKING
YOUR OWN

Illustration: Ned Selby

34

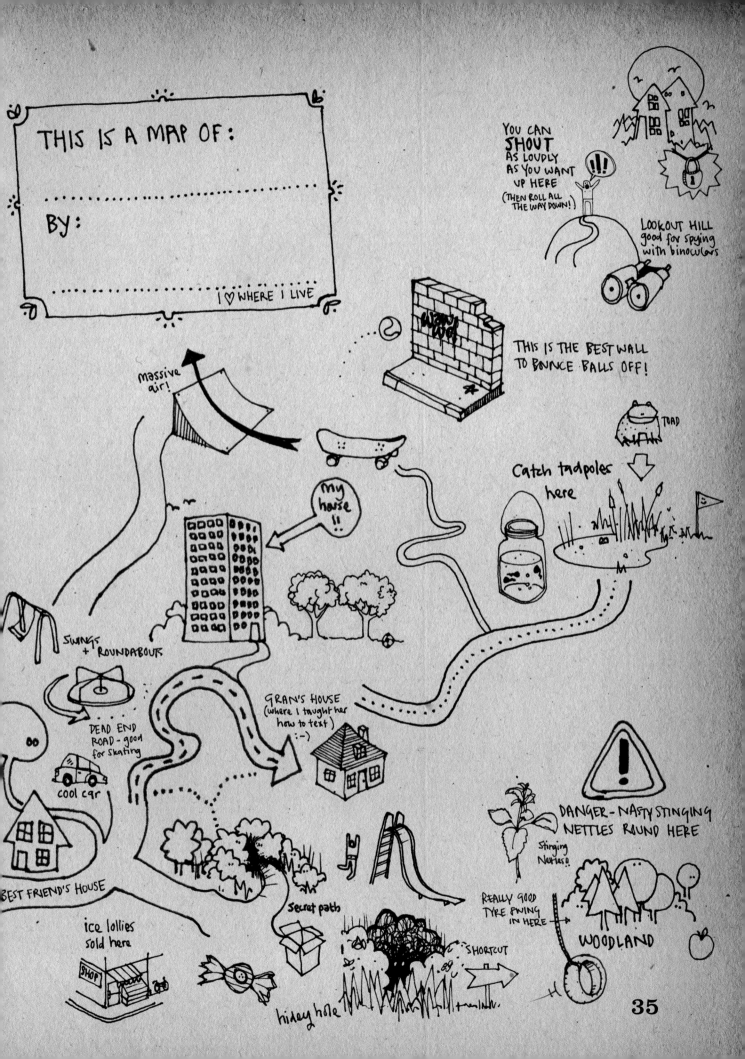

THIS IS A MAP OF:

....

BY:

....

I ♡ WHERE I LIVE

YOU CAN **SHOUT** AS LOUDLY AS YOU WANT UP HERE (THEN ROLL ALL THE WAY DOWN!)

LOOKOUT HILL good for spying with binoculars

THIS IS THE BEST WALL TO BOUNCE BALLS OFF!

TOAD

Catch tadpoles here

massive air!

my house !!

SWINGS + ROUNDABOUTS

DEAD END ROAD - good for skating

cool car

GRAN'S HOUSE (where I taught her how to text) :-)

DANGER - NASTY STINGING NETTLES ROUND HERE

Stinging Nettles!

BEST FRIEND'S HOUSE

Secret path

REALLY GOOD TYRE SWING IN HERE

WOODLAND

ice lollies sold here

SHOP

hidey hole

SHORTCUT

Teach Your Granny to Text

HBTU = Happy Birthday to you

H2CUS = Hope to see you soon

HNTUG = Haven't you grown!

HUH = Have you heard?

AB = Ah bless

B4N = Bye for now

BION = Believe it or not

TYVM = Thank you very much

PCM = *Please call me*   **DGTG** = *Don't go there girlfriend*

L8R = *Later*   **ROTFL** = *Rolling on the floor laughing*

YR = *Yeah, right!*   **KUTGW** = *Keep up the good work*

ZZZZ = *Bored, tired*   **J2LYK** = *Just to let you know*

WFM = *Works for me*   **MTE** = *My thoughts exactly*

VWD = *Very well done*   **FDLSTX** = *Fiddlesticks*

IVKTDUSMLUVLISOX = *I've*   **RUOK** = *Are you OK?*

knitted you some lovely socks   **GR8** = *Great*

:-) = *Happy*   :-D = *Laughing*   :-(= *Sad*   <:-o = *Shocked*

:-o = *Amazed*   %-) = *Confused*   :-~(= *I have a cold*   ;-) = *Wink*

Find out about your food

Our food had a whole life before it reached our table. What's your apple's life story?

I never had what you would call my own room. I grew up on an English "farm" with 30,000 other chickens. I can tell you, it's good preparation for being in a chicken sandwich, being squashed up with that lot. I hear there are other farms where chickens get more space. To perch, peck, cluck about. I dunno. Sounds egg-straordinary to me.

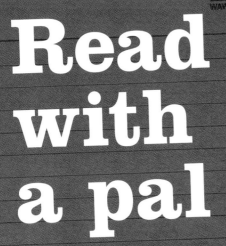

Read with a pal

It's just plain rude to keep a good Alex Rider story all to yourself...

SECRET WEAPON
© Anthony Horowitz

The man with the two missing teeth had thought a great deal about killing Alex Rider. He had imagined it. He had planned it. Today he was going to do it.

His name was Skoda. At least, that was what he had called himself when he had been a drug dealer in west London. He had sold his little packets of death in pubs, at street corners and outside schools until the day he had made just one mistake. He had chosen Brookland School and that was how he had met Alex.

Skoda thought about that as he sat outside the school, 10 months later, watching and waiting. It still seemed impossible. He had been living on a canal boat. The 14-year-old schoolboy had used a crane to hook the boat out of the water and had dropped it – from a height – into the middle of a police conference. Skoda had been arrested immediately. Worse than that; he had become a laughing stock throughout the criminal world. Skoda doubted that Alex would recognize him now. He still had the missing teeth and pierced ears. But the incident with the canal boat had left terrible scars. They had patched him up in hospital but the stitch marks still showed. They began high on his forehead, ran the length of his nose, continued through his mouth and ended under his chin. The two halves of his face had been sewn back together by a doctor who

had obviously never trained in cosmetic surgery. He looked hideous.

But Alex Rider would pay. Skoda had escaped from the prison hospital. He had made enquiries and he had finally discovered who he had to blame for his misfortunes. He knew he would be arrested again eventually. But that didn't matter.

Today it would be his turn to laugh.

Alex was coming out of drama when he ran into the new teacher … literally. He was in a crowd of half a dozen boys and they were all breaking one of the 10 commandments of Brookland School: thou shalt not run in the corridors.

Somehow the others managed to get out of her way. Alex crashed into her.

Everyone had been talking about June Summers since she had arrived, just a few weeks ago. She was a supply teacher – physics and chemistry – and suddenly everyone wanted to do science. Miss Summers was young, still in her 20s, and almost absurdly attractive with blonde hair falling to her shoulders, amazing blue eyes and movie star lips. She dressed like a teacher with a grey, tailored jacket and serious shoes. But she walked like a model. The boys joked about her. And Alex had just run into her. It was the first time they'd met.

"Good morning," she said. "I'm Miss Summers."

"I'm sorry…" Alex bent down and picked up her papers for her.

She looked at him coolly. "You're Alex Rider," she said.

"Yes." He wondered how she knew.

"I've been looking at your reports from last term. You've got a lot of catching up to do."

"I was away … sick."

"You seem to get sick a lot," Miss Summers said.

Alex couldn't tell her the truth. He couldn't tell anyone. Even if he had been allowed to, nobody would have believed him.

He had no parents. He had been brought up by an uncle – Ian Rider – who had been a spy, working in an obscure department of MI6 … a secret within a secret. Then his uncle had died and somehow they had manipulated Alex into taking his place. There were times, they had said, when a child could achieve things that an adult could not. And if he missed school? If he came back each time, not just injured but with his whole life bent out of shape? It didn't matter. He was doing it for his country. Nobody must know.

Of course, Miss Summers was right. Despite his efforts to catch up, Alex was slipping behind in class. She had read his reports. His form teacher: "Alex is a bright and pleasant boy but he would be doing much better if he turned up more regularly at school…"

And humanities: "Alex needs to join in more and to be part of the class. He was absent again this term. But he wrote a first-class essay on Russian politics and the collapse of the fleet at Murmansk."

That had amused Alex. What he'd learned about Murmansk hadn't come out of a book. If it hadn't been for him, Murmansk – along with half of Russia – would no longer exist.

Miss Summers was still watching him with those deep, blue eyes. "Are you going on the trip this afternoon?" she asked.

"Yes, Miss."

"Are you interested in weapons?"

Alex thought briefly of all the guns and knives that, at different times, had been aimed at him. "Yes," he said.

"Well enjoy it. But don't run in the corridor."

She took back her papers and then she was gone, brushing past him and disappearing into the staff room. Alex wondered what she did when she wasn't working as a supply teacher. A bell rang. Walking fast, he headed for the next class.

The exhibition at the British Museum was called Seven Hundred Years of War and had hundreds of weapons – from medieval bows to automatic machine guns – displayed in a dozen galleries. Two classes from Brookland had gone, with Miss Summers and Mr Bryce (who taught history) in charge. It was the last visit of the day. The museum was about to close.

Later, Alex would be unsure quite how he had managed to lag behind. He had been looking at a case of replica guns. MI6 never let him have a gun. Maybe that was why he was interested. At the same time, he had become aware of a security guard showing the other visitors out of the gallery, before slowly walking over to him. The guard seemed to have been involved in a bad car accident. His face was divided by a line of stitches.

"Enjoying yourself?" the guard asked.

Alex shrugged.

"If you like weapons, you might be interested in this one."

The guard smiled and that was what saved Alex. The two missing teeth. Instantly, Alex knew he had seen the man before – and he was already moving, sliding backwards as the fake guard suddenly produced a vicious sword, taken from the kung fu gallery next door. It was a unicorn sword, also called lin jiao dao, 15th century, Chinese. It had three razor-sharp blades: one about a metre long and the others shorter, attached to the handle and shaped like lethal crescent moons. The guard had aimed for his head. As Alex leapt back, he actually felt the sword slice the air, less than a centimetre from his face.

The guard came at him a second time, stabbing forward now with the three blades. Alex only just managed to avoid them, hampered by his school uniform and backpack. He twisted back, lost his balance and fell. He heard the man laugh out loud as his shoulders crashed into the wooden floor and the breath was knocked out of him.

The guard walked forward, spinning the sword. That was when Alex remembered his name.

"Skoda!" he said.

"You remember me?"

"I never forget a face. But something seems to have happened to yours."

Alex tried to get up but Skoda pushed him back with the sole of his foot.

"You did this to me," he snarled and Alex saw that the two halves of his head no longer worked at the same time. It was as if two people were fighting for control of his mouth. "And now you're going to pay!" Skoda giggled. "This is going to be slow. This is going to hurt!"

He raised the sword. There was nothing Alex could do. For once, he was helpless, on his back – with no gadgets, no clever moves. Skoda took a breath. He was like a butcher examining a prime cut of meat. His tongue hung out. It was also stitched in two halves. There was a soft thudding sound. Skoda pitched forward and lay still. There was a small, feathered dart sticking out of his neck. Alex looked past him and his head swam. Miss Summers was standing there, holding a tranquilliser gun.

"Are you hurt, Alex?" she asked.

Alex got unsteadily to his feet. "You...?" he began. He was staring at the gun.

"It's all right," Miss Summers said. "I'm with MI6." She touched the unconscious drug dealer with the tip of her shoe. "We knew Skoda had escaped. We were afraid he might come after you. I was sent in to keep an eye on you."

"You're a spy?"

"I think the words you're looking for are – thank you!"

It was true. She had just saved his life. Alex looked around him. Seven hundred years of war. He was part of it now and had been ever since his uncle had died. MI6 had made him their secret weapon. They had put him into a glass case of their own and they were the ones with the key.

"Thank you, Miss Summers," he said.

"Don't mention it, Alex," Miss Summers replied. "Now, you'd better go down and find the others while I deal with our friend." She smiled at him. "And try to remember not to run!"

Don't sing in the shower

The average shower lasts seven minutes and uses 35 litres of water.

Actually, two minutes is all it takes to soap up, wash down, scrub your armpits, do your rude bits and still have time for your hair. If everyone in your class took two minute showers for a year, with the water saved you could fill an entire swimming pool. And then some.

Take shorter showers. Save your singing for the rain.

(PS Shorter showers also mean longer lie-ins. Which is almost as good as saving the world.)

Illustration: Andrew Wightman

Play

OK, so we lied.
Not all of the actions are in
the book. This one's outside.
Waiting to happen.

Photography: New Future Graphic

You still here? Go play!

Give lots of compliments

Compliments get easier when you do them regularly. So make a 5-a-day habit of giving them away. They cost nothing. They make you feel good. Everyone accepts them. And a good one can last for weeks.

B·D·C

1

B·D·C BANQUE DE COMPLIMENTS   *give one get one free!*

TO:.. DATE ....

COMPLIMENT: ....

....

SIGNED ....

2

B·D·C BANQUE DE COMPLIMENTS   *give one get one free!*

TO:.. DATE ....

COMPLIMENT: ....

....

SIGNED ....

3

B·D·C BANQUE DE COMPLIMENTS   *give one get one free!*

TO:.. DATE ....

COMPLIMENT: ....

....

SIGNED ....

4

B·D·C BANQUE DE COMPLIMENTS   *give one get one free!*

TO:.. DATE ....

COMPLIMENT: ....

....

SIGNED ....

5

B·D·C BANQUE DE COMPLIMENTS   *give one get one free!*

TO:.. DATE ....

COMPLIMENT: ....

....

SIGNED ....

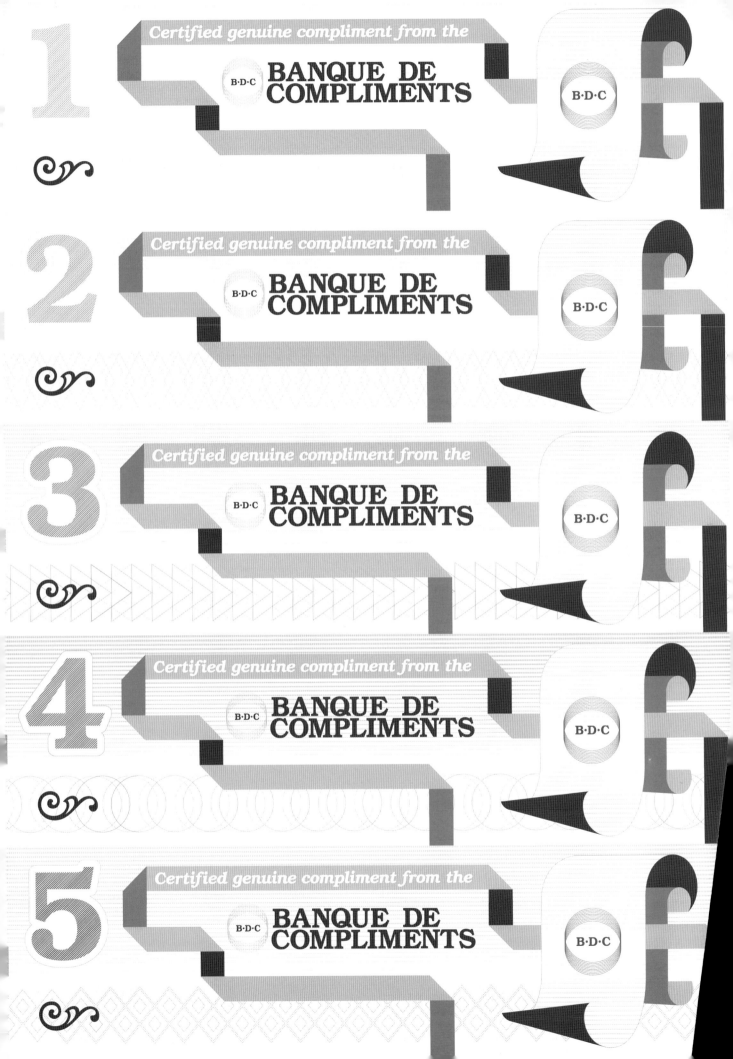

1

BANQUE DE COMPLIMENTS B·D·C *give one get one free!*

TO: Samantha   DATE Monday

COMPLIMENT:

I like your hair

SIGNED Selan

2

BANQUE DE COMPLIMENTS B·D·C *give one get one free!*

TO: Noah   DATE march 2

COMPLIMENT: you are good
in goal

SIGNED Sam

3

BANQUE DE COMPLIMENTS B·D·C *give one get one free!*

TO: cara thornton   DATE monday

COMPLIMENT: I Like sitting
Next to you

SIGNED Sophie B.

4

BANQUE DE COMPLIMENTS B·D·C *give one get one free!*

TO: Mohammed   DATE June 1

COMPLIMENT:

You look happy

SIGNED Tahir

5

BANQUE DE COMPLIMENTS B·D·C *give one get one free!*

TO: Cara   DATE 21/3

COMPLIMENT: you make me laugh

SIGNED Eugenie

Stop junk mail

Don't charge your phone overnight

SLAM DUNK THE JUNK NO JUNK MAIL

I'M JUNK FREE, ME!

JUNK

I ♥ TREES

no junk mail please

Use this sticker for your own design

SLAM DUNK THE JUNK NO JUNK MAIL

My letter box is on a diet - NO JUNK MAIL PLEASE

I'M JUNK FREE, ME!

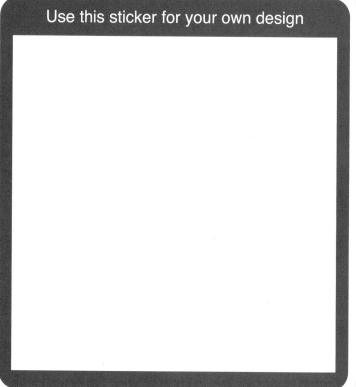

Use this sticker for your own design

I ♥ TREES

no junk mail please

By putting a "no junk mail" sign on your letter box you can cut junk mail by around 90 per cent.

Stick us on your door. And share us with the neighbours :-)

Sorry. Extra energy doesn't equal extra whizzy super powers (nice as that would be).

Most mobile phones are fully charged in under two hours. But in Britain we waste £47 million a year charging them all night.

Don't. We all need our zzz's. That includes you, Mobie.

Illustration: Nigel Coan

Don't start a war

We make 216 choices every day. Try and make the right ones.

Illustrations: Jim Medway

RING! RING!

BUMP!

OUFF!

OI, KELLY! WATCH WHERE YOU'RE GOING!

SORRY MATE!

DON'T BOTHER, I DON'T WANT YOUR SMELLY MITTS ON MY STUFF!

SMELLY KELLY!

SHOVE!

BACK AT HOME —

MR KELLY'S COMING ROUND. WHAT'S THIS *RUN-IN* WITH HIS SON?

CLICK!

TIM KELLY SMACKED INTO ME ON PURPOSE, THEN THEY ALL STARTED ON HIM. IT WASN'T MY FAULT!

DING DONG!

TIM GOT BEATEN UP TODAY. I'D LIKE A WORD WITH YOUR BOY ABOUT IT.

HAH! YOUR SON STARTED IT!

YOUR SON'S A *BULLY!*

YOURS IS A *THUG!*

IF YOU THINK THIS IS THE END OF IT, YOU'RE WRONG...

...TOMORROW THIS GOES TO THE HEADMASTER...

I WISH WE'D NEVER MOVED HERE!

YOU'VE GONE THE *WRONG* WAY ABOUT MAKING FRIENDS, I CAN TELL YOU...

≈SIGH≈

CLEARLY, THIS IS ONLY THE BEGINNING...

Don't worry if you make a mistake

(sometimes these things have a way of working out...)

It was 1886 and pharmacist John Pemberton just couldn't get his magical medicine to work. It was supposed to cure tiredness and sore teeth but about the only thing going for it was that it tasted good. It was Coca-Cola. Which now sells a billion drinks a day.

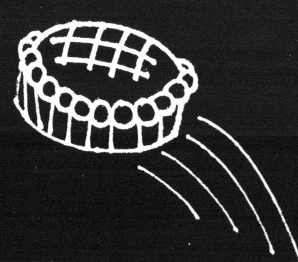

When little Frank Epperson was asked to stir a fruit drink by his mum in 1905, he thought better of it and went off to play. It stood overnight on the porch.

Some college students in America so loved the Frisbie Pies from the famous Frisbie Bakery that they would not only eat them, but play with the tins afterwards. Their favourite game was throwing pie dishes to each other yelling "Frisbie" to warn others.
It caught on.

By morning it had frozen stiff with the spoon stuck straight up. Frank was in trouble. And the world had the popsicle.

In 1928, Scottish scientist Alexander Fleming left an experiment by an open window. By morning his bacteria samples had gone mouldy. But instead of throwing them out, he looked closer and found that the mould was gradually dissolving the harmful bacteria. Turns out he'd only gone and discovered penicillin - the wonder antibiotic used to save billions of lives.

In 1853 New York there was a very picky customer. And a very grumpy chef. The customer demanded that his potatoes be cut thinner and fried longer. Furious, the chef cut them very thin, fried them for ages and covered them in salt. The customer asked for more. Hooray! The crisp was born.

Christopher Columbus was an explorer looking for Asia. But in 1492 he sailed the wrong way and ended up in an entirely different continent. Happily for him, he didn't realise at the time and announced, quite smugly, that, ho hum, here he was in Asia. And so it was that America was discovered.

Walking across deserts is thirsty work. So, hundreds of years ago, an Arabian merchant had an idea. He'd carry his precious milk in a pouch made from a sheep's stomach. But chemicals from the pouch and the heat of the desert turned the milk into cheese. Lovely on toast. Crummy if you want a drink.

Walking on a ship deck in 1943 an engineer watched, interested, as a coiled spring fell to the floor and sort of slinked around. Hmm. He thought. Later he and his wife made their own spiral at home, dropped it from the top step and watched it slinky-dink down to the bottom step. Of almost every house in America.

Talk rubbish to your parents

Next time your parents say "Haven't you cleaned your room?", say "I'm glad you brought that up. I've been meaning to talk to you about cleaning up your habits!"

Glass bottles are totally recyclable. But in landfill they will never decompose

60%
amount of recyclable rubbish in our bins

TIP: you can find out more at www.recyclenow.com

Write a letter

Reasons why a letter can be better:

You can't put a text message on the wall.
You can't re-read a phone conversation.
Who ever heard of a love-email?

PS
Of course you could call. Or send a text.
But everyone loves a letter.

Dear Friend / Enemy / Politician / Mum

I thought that I should write to you to say that: you owe me money / I'd like to be friends / I will not stand for global warming / I owe you money.

The situation is less than ideal and from now on I will be: chasing you / not chasing you / writing to you every day / begging your forgiveness.

I hope you understand that I am: skint / keen to make a new start / a future taxpayer/ your only child.

Lots of love

Me

Recycle your toys

There are around 400 million
forgotten toys in the UK.
Unused. Unloved. Under the bed.
It doesn't have to be this way.
Take them to a charity shop.
Give them away. Swap them.

Love your toys. And when you're
done lovin', set them free.

There's life in
the old bear yet

卌 卌 卌
卌 卌 卌
卌 卌 卌
卌 卌 卌
卌 卌 |||

Involve everyone

Some things work better when you do them with lots and lots of people – Mexican waves, football matches, changing the world.

This action is one of those things.

Create a story full of interesting twists and turns by adding just three words and then passing it on to someone else. The more people you get involved, the better the story gets.

We've written the first three for you.

(The only tricky bit is making sure your story ends at the same place as the page!)

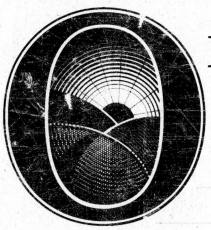NCE THERE WAS...

Finished the story? Don't keep it to yourself! Log onto
www.wearewhatwedo.org and tell the world (wide web)

63

Speak football

CIAO

SA

ADAAB

HELLO

Yes, you're right. Football is a game and not a language. Silly us.

But kicking a ball around is a great way of talking to people who might not understand you.

HOLA

There are 6,000 languages in the world. Football speaks every one of them.

WUNMAN NJINDE

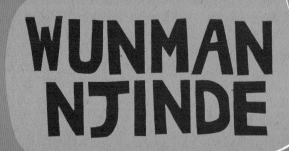

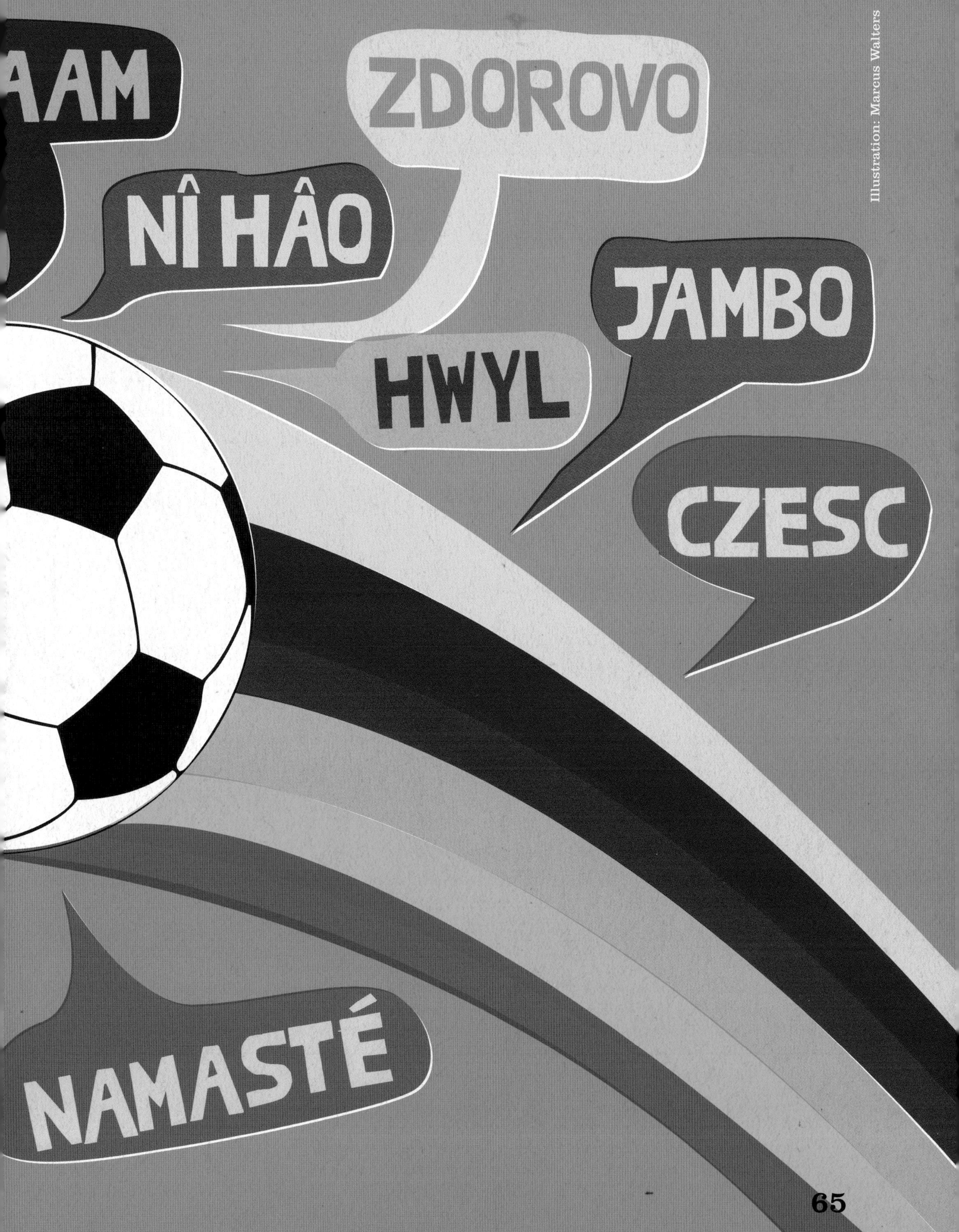

Illustration: Marcus Walters

Add your own action

Oh thank goodness you're here. We've been waiting for you. Holding your page. You see we're one author short of a book. One action short too. And it's the most important, because it's yours.

So. What's the one thing you would ask one million people to do to change the world? Take your time (writers always do). Then go tell all your friends you've just finished writing your first book.

I'd like one million people to...

Added your action?
Don't keep it to yourself.
Log onto www.wearewhatwedo.org
and tell the world.

This book started with a question...

"What would you ask one million people to do to change the world?"

We asked every child in the country. And got thousands of answers.

Some were sensible actions, some were super-actions, some were just plain bonkers but we loved every one of them. We wished we could have included them all. But that would have been way too many pages for a book. So we asked kids, teachers, parents, even a few celebs to pick their favourites and, hey presto, out came 30 blinders. Great minds think alike – lots of you had the same idea (more or less). Others were complete one-offs.

Everyone who contributed actions made this book. Just like everyone who reads it, and adds **their** own action, makes this book. To all of you, the true authors of this book. A huge thank you.

Action 01: Make someone smile
Rebecca Dixon, Elif Wright, Emma Dixon, Gilwern Primary School, Gwent. **With thanks:** Colin Welch; Tom McKee, Whitehead Primary School, County Antrim; Ellie Eastwood, Kain Bovel, Jordan Grimes, Britney Macklin, Elise Lima, Zac Hayward, Ellacombe School, Devon; Hannah Edgar, Danielle Heighington, Dereham Neatherd High School, Norfolk; Luisha Grant, All Hallows RC Business and Enterprise College, Lancashire.

Action 02: Walk your dad
Cato Tallis-Lock and Edward Prendeville, Godwin Junior School, London.

Action 03: Grow something & eat it
Grace Abbotts, Staffordshire; Sunneka Deocampo, St Andrew's CE Primary School, East Sussex; Katie Laurilla, Georgia Stephenson, Duke Kent, Oliver Wells, Sapphire Hodder, Jenny Baldwin, Fiona Salisbury, Ringwood School, Hampshire.

Action 04: Stand up for something
Adan, London; Anthony Puricelli, St Matthew's Academy, London; Sabirul Islam, City and Islington Sixth Form College, London.

Action 05: Switch things off when you leave the room
Kian Stevens, St Theresa's Catholic Primary School, Sheffield. **With thanks:** Energy Savings Trust.

Action 06: Test your teacher
Lois Zac-Williams and Ben McMullan, Godwin Junior School, London.
With thanks: Westgate School, Lancashire.

Action 07: Look closer
Geoffrey Kenworthy, Calverton Primary School.

Action 08: Be friendly in sign language
The children at Community Links Southern Road After School Club, London. **With thanks:** John Smith, Deaf Comedian (www.beautifulbsl.co.uk), Royal National Institute of the Deaf.

Action 09: Layer up
Hollie Evans, St Andrew's CE Primary School. **With thanks:** Charlotte Ellis, St Mary's First School, West Sussex.

Action 10: Cook a meal from scratch
Liam Wilkinson, Kim Wilkinson, Adam Ogden, Chloe Hardwicke, Katie Lodge, Amy Bennett, Danielle Knight, Charlotte Smith, Abi Gray, Hannah Quinn, The Billericay School, Essex. **With thanks:** Genevieve Herr, Ellen Holgate.

Action 11: Love your stuff
Sophia Jones, Ringwood School, Hampshire and Imogen Strachan, St Thomas' Clapham, London. **With thanks:** The stuff loving children from Godwin Junior School, London, and St Mary's First School, West Sussex.

Action 12: Go to more parties
St Angela's Ursuline School, London and Merchant Taylors Junior School, Stanfield.

Action 13: Ask "Why?"
Serena Parekh, Roxeth First and Middle School, Middlesex. **With thanks:** Essex Road Primary School, London and Sam Elliott, St Mary's First School, West Sussex.

Action 14: Love where you live
Jessie Robinson, New Vic Newham Sixth Form College, London.

Action 15: Teach your granny to text
Erica Ritchie, St John the Baptist School, London.

Action 16: Find out about your food
Year 8 students, St Angela's Ursuline School, London. **With thanks:** The Royal Society for the Prevention of Cruelty to Animals

Action 17: Read with a pal
Christchurch Primary, Hannah Richardson, St Mark's Catholic Primary School, Suffolk. **With thanks:** Joshua Dunser, Precious Meshe, Anthony George, Amy Gabriel, Kyra Crawford-Registe, Sorcha Boyle, Juanita Mwaniki, Grace Crawford, Tamara Brown, Christoher Harnett, Sian Madge, Cordelia Oware, St Winefride's Primary School, London.

Action 18: Don't sing in the shower
Mystery student at The Billericay School, Essex (the search continues).

Action 19: Play
Bill Hillier, London. **With thanks:** Alby and Remy D'Rozario-Gray, London.

Action 20: Give lots of compliments
Emma Desouza, Ashlawn Sixth Form, Rugby.

Action 21: Stop junk mail
Tom Geall, St Mary's First School, West Sussex.

Action 22 - Don't charge your phone overnight
Sammah Shariff, Tollgate Primary School, London. With thanks: Energy Savings Trust.

Action 23: Don't start a war
Jone Yen, Gateway Primary School, London.

Action 24: Don't worry if you make a mistake
Joe Robinson, St Bonaventures, London.

Action 25: Talk rubbish to your parents
A big thank you to the hundreds of children that came up with ideas about recycling, with a special mention to: Kaine Wild, St Theresa's Catholic Primary School, South Yorkshire; Sophie Wildgoose, St Joseph's RC Primary School, South Yorkshire; Iona Connelly, Clara Smith, Thomas' Clapham, London; Callum Minns, St Mark's Catholic Primary School, Suffolk; Joey Walsworth, St Mary's First School, West Sussex.

Action 26: Write a letter
Ringwood School, Hampshire. **With thanks:** Royal Mail.

Action 27: Recycle your toys
Hannah Richardson, St Mark's Catholic Primary School, Suffolk. **With thanks:** Joshua Dunser, Precious Meshe, Anthony George, Amy Gabriel, Kyra Crawford-Registe, Sorcha Boyle, Juanita Mwaniki, Grace Crawford, Tamara Brown, Christopher Hartnett, Sian Madge, Cordelia Oware, St Winefride's Primary School, London; Kinza Khan, Christchurch Primary.

Action 28: Involve everyone
Everyone (obviously) at Hessle High School, East Yorkshire, and in particular Amy Rose, Laura Pryor, Joe Bradywood, Adam Mullarkey, Daniel Crawley, Lewis Henery, Caitlin Harvey, Megan Gray, Jenni Leeman. **With thanks:** Lowri and Nia Thomas, Cwmtawe Comprehensive, Pontardawe; Jessie-May Wilson, Tottenhall Infant School, London; Ryan Brown, Ringwood School, Hampshire.

Action 29: Speak football
Omar Bynon, Godwin Junior School, London.

Action 30 – Add your own action
You!

Little bit wacky
(but how we loved you...)

There were fights. There were tears. But not all of our favourite actions could make it into the top thirty. We fondly remember:

Recycle a rabbit "I got my rabbit from a rabbit rescue centre in Greenwich. Rabbit rescue centres look after rabbits that have been disowned and then find kind and good owners to care for them. My rabbit is called Mumble." Becca

Save your hair "Save your hair when you go for a haircut and then give it to a bald person to keep them warm in the winter." Sapphire

Thank you

Lots of people helped us with this book and to each and every one we say "thank you". In particular, we would like to thank:

The Department for Children, Schools and Families (DCSF) for funding, support and trust. Without the DCSF this book would never have been written. In particular, thank you to Janice Lawson, David Serrant and Jake Reynolds.

The Times for their support, ideas, energy and enthusiasm. In particular, Hilly Janes and Anna Shepard.

Short Books our dear old friends, Rebecca Nicolson, Aurea Carpenter, Catherine Gibbs, Vanessa Webb and Emily Fox.

Walker Books our new friends, Jane Winterbotham, Ben Norland, Beth Aves, Alan Lee, Jane Harris, Anya Hollis, Corinne Gotch, Caroline Royds and Genevieve Herr.

New Future Graphic for their never-ending patience, good humour and skill – Marcus Walters, Gareth White and Ned Selby.

Special thanks to the thousands of teachers, schools, youth workers and young people who have helped us in developing our work with young people. In particular, Helen Matthews, Lois Stokes, Scilla Morgan, Jenny Beeching, Jenny Wilks, Fidelma Boyd, Paul Jackson, Dave Smithers, Tom Canning, Zuhayb Ahmed – the Newham Youth Mayor, Steve Wilks, Peg Probert, Ishlal Lawrence, Jane Ray, Kate Phillips, Isclal Lawrence and Sudell Primary School, Darwen. Selah Nyamambi, Cara Thornton, English Martyrs School, Holmleigh Primary School, Romsey School.

We are also very grateful to the following organisations which have supported the launch of the We Are What We Do Young Speakers Programme: **The Aldridge Foundation**, the youth volunteering charity *v* and the national volunteering charity **TimeBank**. Very special thanks to Rodney Aldridge OBE for his vision and passion as well as Sally Ritchie, Nigel Mansfield, Andrew Dick, Helen Platt and Brendan Loughran.

A movement for global change doesn't happen without a lot of friends and supporters. We thank every single one of you, and in particular…

Accenture Gavin Rennie, David French, Siobhain McCullagh, Julika Erfurt, Andrew James; **Allen & Overy LLP** Shankari Chandran, Natalie Behrman, Richard Browne, Colin Pearson, Sarah Marquis, Catriona Smith, Ceris Gardner, Sophie Mazzer, Emma-Jane Weider, Kirralee Sanders, Deidre Moynihan; **BDO Stoy Hayward** Jeremy Newman, Marios Brooks, Jo Dooley, Debbie Fields; **Brunswick Group LLP** Alan Parker, Frank Villaz; **CAN** Adele Blakebrough, Andrew Croft; **Community Links** Max Weaver, Jane Parish, Richard McKeever, Gordon Lane; **Good Business** Giles Gibbons, Alex Tredgett; **Lyndales Solicitors** Stanley Harris, Anne Prytherch; **Nipple** Nigel Coan; **Newham Recorder; One Aldwych** and Gordon Campbell Gray; **Sainsbury's** Justin King, Gwyn Burr, Jat Sahota; **Sainsbury's Trust; Stratford Development Partnership Charitable Trust** Stephen Jacobs; **Teach First** Sarah Higgs, Malachi McIntosh; **The Teaching Awards** Sophie Byatt; **The Book Service** Richard Hoban; **SVP Communications; The Early Learning Centre, Saatchi&Saatchi, BBH, Innocent.**

And not forgetting…

Fiona Harrison, Matthew Smerdon, Eliza Anderson, Frauke Godat, Paul Edney, Gordon Rae, Mark Blackwell, Jenny Heller, Linda Woolston, Nicki Kennedy, Phil Solomon, Anne Shewring, Tim Ashton, Steve Henry, Sophie Lewis, Nicholla Longley, Russell Davies, Yusuf Chuku, Rose Wangen-Jones, Eoghain Clarke, Graham Pritchard, Julian Andrews, Steve Wish, Teresa Wickam, Lucy Read, Nicola Berry, Spyros Zevelakis, Kate Taylor, Elis Matthews, Adil Abrar, Andrew Bell, Martin Collier, Laura Deeley, Rebecca Gibbs, Tracey Kiddle, Chris Holmes, Dr Helen Marshall, Mark Triggs, Colette Harvey, Joel Joffe, Christian Strasser, Ronnie Corbett, Dermot O'Leary, Paul Jackson, Sophie Lewis, Nicholla Longley. And last but by no means least, James Alexander, for eighteen months of tireless work as a volunteer, mentor and dear friend to We Are What We Do.

We Are What We Do team - **Eugenie Harvey, James Alexander, David Robinson, David Brook, Nick Stanhope, Nicole van den Eijnde, Roger Granada, Zoe Cameron, Sandra Deeble, Sam Bond, Tanis Taylor and Frances Clarke.**